I

LOVE

YOU

summersdale

An Hachette UK Company
www.hachette.co.uk

Summersdale Publishers Ltd
Part of Octopus Publishing Group Limited
Carmelite House
50 Victoria Embankment
LONDON
EC4Y 0DZ
UK

www.summersdale.com

Printed and bound in China

ISBN: 978-1-80007-025-7

Substantial discounts on bulk quantities of Summersdale books are available to corporations, professional associations and other organizations. For details contact general enquiries: telephone: +44 (0) 1243 771107 or email: enquiries@summersdale.com.

To..

From.......................................

In all the world, there is no love for you like mine.

Maya Angelou

I'd like to paint
you, but there
are no colours,
because there
are so many, in
my confusion, the
tangible form of
my great love.

Frida Kahlo

It was
always you

Why, darling,
I don't live at
all when I'm
not with you.

Ernest Hemingway

I've tried so many
times to think
of a new way to
say it, and it's
still I love you.

Zelda Fitzgerald

It's an unexplainable feeling, an expression. It's a touch, it's a feel. Once you feel it, it's like no other thing in the world.

Snoop Dogg on love

You are my
forever love

I love him to hell and back and heaven and back, and have and do and will.

Sylvia Plath

There is only
one happiness in
this life, to love
and be loved.

George Sand

When I met you,
I found me

Love loves
to love love.

James Joyce

It is incredible
how essential
to me you have
become.

Vita Sackville-West

Gamble
everything for
love, if you
are a true
human being.

Rumi

When we love
we can let our
hearts speak.

bell hooks

Love makes you go places you probably wouldn't ever go, had it not been for love.

Rihanna

We'll cling together so tight that nothing and no one'll ever tear us apart. Every atom of me and every atom of you.

Philip Pullman

Between your own desire and my desire the space is starry, each step quakes the ground...

Federico García Lorca

My heart
chose you

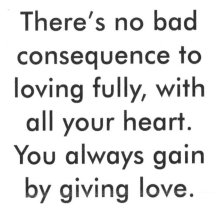

There's no bad consequence to loving fully, with all your heart. You always gain by giving love.

Reese Witherspoon

Your voice is my
favourite sound

At Toulouse I simply loved you. Tonight I love you on a spring evening. I love you with the window open.

Jean-Paul Sartre

For me,
love is
endless.

Khalid

You feel like
a dream

I am in love –
and, my God,
it's the greatest
thing that can
happen to a man.

D. H. Lawrence

It's always wrong to hate, but it's never wrong to love.

Lady Gaga

Not loving is but a long dying.

Emperor Wu of Han

A list of reasons
why I love you:

1. You're you

I think the
perfection of
love is that it's
not perfect.

Taylor Swift

If you remember
me, then I don't
care if everyone
else forgets.

Haruki Murakami

I love you
even more
than I loved
you yesterday

One hour of
right-down love
is worth an age of
dully living on.

Aphra Behn

I loved her
against reason,
against promise,
against peace,
against hope,
against happiness,
against all
discouragement
that could be.

Charles Dickens

**Falling in love
is not rational.
It's madness.
A beautiful,
wonderful moment
of magnificent
insanity.**

Michael Faudet

You are my sunshine

Love is divine
only and difficult
always.

Toni Morrison

Love hinders
death. Love is life.
All, everything
that I understand,
I understand only
because I love.

Leo Tolstoy

You set my
soul on fire

It's like time has lost all continuity. Every second with you outweighs days of life before I met you.

Stephanie Meyer

Love doesn't cease; love reshapes.

Iman Bowie

When you find that one that's right for you, you feel like they were put there for you.

Joe Manganiello

I adore you

There is no pretending... I love you.

Cassandra Clare

Soul meets soul
on lovers' lips.

Percy Bysshe Shelley

I'm yours

I saw somebody
and experienced
all of those
things you hear
about in songs
and read about
in poetry. My
knees were weak.

Portia de Rossi

Is it necessary to define love?

Patti Smith

♥

You are my sun, my moon and all my stars.

E. E. Cummings

**This is the
deepest love I've
ever known**

If you find someone you love in your life, then hang on to that love.

Diana, Princess of Wales

Love is just a word until someone comes along and gives it meaning.

Paulo Coelho

To me,
you are
perfect

Love is when you have somebody that doesn't make you give up half of yourself.

Kehlani

I love her,
and that's the
beginning and end
of everything.

F. Scott Fitzgerald

I swear I couldn't love you more than I do right now, and yet I know I will tomorrow.

Leo Christopher

Let's grow
old together

Lots of people want to ride with you in the limo, but what you want is someone who will take the bus with you when the limo breaks down.

Oprah Winfrey

As one needs
happiness so
have I needed
love; that is the
deepest need of
the human spirit.

Rockwell Kent

You make my heart flutter

You pierce my soul. I am half agony, half hope... I have loved none but you.

Jane Austen

Love is space and
time measured
by the heart.

Marcel Proust

To be brave is
to love someone
unconditionally,
without expecting
anything in return.

Madonna

When
you know,
you know

All I love, all I want, all I need is you – forever.

Marilyn Monroe

You come to love
not by finding the
perfect person,
but by seeing
an imperfect
person perfectly.

Sam Keen

You complete me

My love is selfish. I cannot breathe without you.

John Keats

There are
darknesses in life
and there are
lights, and you
are one of the
lights, the light
of all lights.

Bram Stoker

Love is like
a friendship
caught on fire.

Bruce Lee

True love knows
no bounds

I love love.
I'm, like,
obsessed
with it.

Camila Cabello

I want you to laugh,
to kill all your
worries, to love you,
to nourish you.

Rumi

You take my
breath away

The regret of my life is that I have not said "I love you" often enough.

Yoko Ono

Where there is love there is life.

Mahatma Gandhi

Doubt thou the
stars are fire;
Doubt that the
sun doth move;
Doubt truth
to be a liar;
But never
doubt I love.

William Shakespeare

Love unites us

I couldn't say
je t'aime and
je t'adore as
I longed to
do, but always
remember that
I am saying it,
that I go to sleep
thinking of you.

Eleanor Roosevelt

I have decided to stick to love. Hate is too great a burden to bear.

Martin Luther King Jr

You + me = always

Whatever our souls are made of, his and mine are the same.

Emily Brontë

Love is an endless act of forgiveness.

Beyoncé

I wake up every morning thankful that it wasn't all a dream.

Adam Levine

My life,
my lover,
my best friend

I think love is something that you have to work on, and it develops over experience and time. Love is a practice.

Shakira

Where have
you been all
my life?

Nick Jonas

I love you
to the moon
and back

Kindness
eases change.
Love quiets fear.

Octavia E. Butler

I cannot let you burn me up, nor can I resist you. No mere human can stand in a fire and not be consumed.

A. S. Byatt

**To have fallen
in love completely
and unreservedly
makes all one's
personal and
even the world's
troubles seem
small and petty.**

Prince Philip,
Duke of Edinburgh

A true
love story
never ends

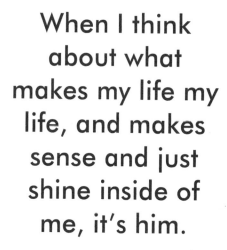

When I think about what makes my life my life, and makes sense and just shine inside of me, it's him.

Julia Roberts

Love is something eternal... the aspect may change, but not the essence.

Vincent van Gogh

I loved you
then and I love
you still

It doesn't matter who you are or what you look like, so long as somebody loves you.

Roald Dahl

I've never had
a moment's doubt.
I love you. I believe in
you completely. You
are my dearest one.
My reason for life.

Ian McEwan

I can live
without money,
but I cannot live
without love.

Judy Garland

You are my
happy place

You have to be prepared to be hurt in order to experience love.

Michaela Coel

I will never forget
the moment I
fell for you

Love is probably
the strongest
emotion that
you can feel...
there's so many
different forms of
it, millions of layers
– you could write
forever about it.

Shawn Mendes

Love is of
all passions
the strongest,
for it attacks
simultaneously the
head, the heart,
and the senses.

Anonymous

Like the rain
fallin' from
the heaven,
it'll come.
Just don't
never give
up on love.

Sonia Sanchez

Personally, I love a great love story.

Meghan, Duchess of Sussex

You are magic

Two people in love, alone, isolated from the world, that's beautiful.

Milan Kundera

I am who I am because of you. You are every reason, every hope, and every dream I've ever had.

Nicholas Sparks

I couldn't bear to
be without you

I can't imagine going on this wild ride with anybody else.

Michelle Obama

Here's to all the places we went. And all the places we'll go. And here's to me, whispering again and again and again and again: I love you.

John Green

Love does
not consist
of gazing at
each other,
but in looking
outward
together in the
same direction.

Antoine de Saint-Exupéry

---❤---

Only you can make
me smile like this

_____

You realize like, "Oh this is like the real thing is. This is what real love is."

Cameron Diaz

Do all things with love.

Og Mandino

To me you are
the world

♥

True love cannot
be found where
it does not
exist, nor can
it be denied
where it does.

Torquato Tasso

You get to choose
who you love
and who you
decide to give
your heart to.

Emma Watson

Love is accepting
people for who
they are and
what they are,
regardless.

Alicia Keys

Then I
met you…

Then there's love.
Then there's like,
"Oh, my goodness. Hi.
Can I talk to you?"

Whoopi Goldberg

The ways we love each other is timeless. It requires trust, honesty, commitment, romance, and physical chemistry.

John Legend

A lifetime is not long enough to love you

I like you very much. Just as you are.

Helen Fielding

The sound of
a kiss is not so
loud as that of a
cannon, but its
echo lasts a great·
deal longer.

Oliver Wendell Holmes Sr

To be in love
is to touch with
a lighter hand.
In yourself
you stretch,
you are well.

Gwendolyn Brooks

Love
conquers
all

The best smell
in the world
is that man
that you love.

Jennifer Aniston

**When I feel
the support that
I have from him,
I feel invincible.**

Emily Blunt

You make my heart skip a beat

**Love is a smoke
made with the
fume of sighs...
A fire sparkling
in lovers' eyes.**

William Shakespeare

All that matters is love.

My heart is full of
you, none other
than you is in
my thoughts, yet
when I seek to say
to you something
not for the world,
words fail me.

Emily Dickinson

There's no substitute for a great love who says, "No matter what's wrong with you, you're welcome at this table."

Tom Hanks

Continue to share your heart with people even if it has been broken.

Amy Poehler

Eventually,
you will come
to understand
that love heals
everything,
and love is
all there is.

Gary Zukav

You're the keeper
of my heart

**Marry someone
who laughs
at the same
things you do.**

J. D. Salinger

Love is when the other person's happiness is more important than your own.

Kylie Jenner

We are all born for love. It is the principle of existence, and its only end.

Benjamin Disraeli

You feel like
coming home

When you're lucky enough to meet your one person, then life takes a turn for the best. It can't get better than that.

John Krasinski

Love takes off
masks that we
fear we cannot
live without and
know we cannot
live within.

James Baldwin

Love will lead
the way

One word frees us
of all the weight
and pain of life.
That word is love.

Sophocles

People should fall in love with their eyes closed. Just close your eyes. Don't look and it's magic.

Andy Warhol

I'm such a firm believer in love.

Dua Lipa

You make my heart happy

It has made me
better loving
you... it has
made me wiser,
and easier,
and brighter.

Henry James

I love you in this
way because
I do not know
any other way
of loving.

Pablo Neruda

Love with
all your heart
and soul

Vulnerability is the essence of romance. It's the art of being uncalculated, the willingness to look foolish.

Ashton Kutcher

Is love this safety I feel in our silences? Is it this belonging, this completeness?

Chimamanda Ngozi Adichie

In case you ever
foolishly forget:
I am never not
thinking of you.

Virginia Woolf

We loved with a love that was more than love.

Edgar Allan Poe

You are my
heart, my life,
my one and
only thought.

Arthur Conan Doyle

I love you

Have you enjoyed this book?
If so, find us on Facebook at
Summersdale Publishers, on Twitter
at **@Summersdale** and on Instagram
at **@summersdalebooks** and get in
touch. We'd love to hear from you!

www.summersdale.com